97 ORCHARD STREET, NEW YORK

Stories of Immigrant Life

LINDA GRANFIELD

With Photographs by

ARLENE ALDA

LOWER EAST SIDE TENEMENT MUSEUM

TUNDRA BOOKS

For Kathy Lowinger,
who knows the immigrant's voyage of dreams
– L.G.

∼

To the memory of my parents,
who made it better for their children
– A.A.

Text copyright © 2001 by Linda Granfield

Photographs copyright © 2001 by Arlene Alda, unless otherwise noted

Published in Canada by Tundra Books,
481 University Avenue, Toronto, Ontario M5G 2E9

Published in the United States by Tundra Books of Northern
New York, P.O. Box 1030, Plattsburgh, New York 12901

Library of Congress Control Number: 2001087787

National Library of Canada Cataloguing in Publication Data

Granfield, Linda
   97 Orchard Street, New York : stories of immigrant life

ISBN 0-88776-580-7

1. Immigrants – New York (State) – New York – Juvenile literature.
2. Tenement houses – New York (State) – New York – Juvenile
literature. 3. 97 Orchard Street (New York, N.Y.) – Juvenile literature.
I. Alda, Arlene, 1933– .   II. Title. III. Title: Ninety seven
Orchard Street.

F128.9.A1G72 2001   j305.90691097471   C2001-930373-4

We acknowledge the support of the Canada Council for the
Arts and the Ontario Arts Council for our publishing program.

We acknowledge the financial support of the Government of Canada
through the Book Publishing Industry Development Program for our
publishing activities.

Printed and bound in Canada

1 2 3 4 5 6   06 05 04 03 02 01

For decades before Liberty's torch shone on the waters of New York harbor, they came by the thousands across the sea. Frightened, confident, hopeful, seasick, they clutched their many children, few belongings, and countless memories and stepped into America.

For many immigrants, life in the land of promise meant crowded living conditions and a daily struggle to survive. While some were defeated by the misery, others carried on to build a new and better life for themselves and their children in their adopted land. To this day, immigrants continue this voyage of hope and life of determination.

Turn the doorknob and enter the darkened hall of 97 Orchard Street, New York. Its stairways echo with the voices, sobs, and laughter of the thousands of immigrants who made the long journey from their past into their future. Here are some of their stories – our stories.

The hum of her treadle sewing machine stops as Nathalie Gumpertz listens. The creaking wooden hall floors are quiet for a moment – and the whisperers are loud. They're talking about her husband again. "Has he returned?" asks a woman. Nathalie hears no reply. She lifts the soft blue fabric from her lap and trims the seam. Once again, her feet begin to push the treadle. The needle hurries along the cloth, and Nathalie is lulled by the machine's gentle whirring.

The tenants at 97 Orchard Street, in New York's Lower East Side, know that Julius Gumpertz walked out of the building, headed for work, on a crisp October morning in 1874. He has never returned.

Some think that he's been the victim of a robbery, killed for the few coins in his pocket. Others whisper that he has simply abandoned his family and "gone West." Nearly one hundred men a week were leaving their families during the economic depression that gripped America in the mid-1870s. Men's wages had been cut by 30 percent, a quarter of all workers were unemployed, and there was no welfare program to provide aid. For some men, running away seemed to be the only option.

Whatever has happened to Julius, Nathalie has had to find a way to remain at home, caring for her four young children and earning a wage for work done in their cramped rooms. Like thousands of other women, she has become a dressmaker.

OPPOSITE: Nathalie's front room became her "shop," a spot where women came to place orders for clothing alterations. Her sewing machine was set up near the window to give her more light to work by. Seamstresses often suffered from poor eyesight because of inadequate lighting and the large amount of close work their jobs required: sewing hooks and eyes, hand-stitching trims, and making tiny buttonholes.

ABOVE: In Nathalie's time, there were no large department stores where women could select new dresses off the rack. Instead, they took magazine illustrations or their own sketches to local seamstresses to duplicate. Thousands of New York women worked in their homes, snipping patterns and creating the "latest fashions" (which were often taken from out-of-date magazines). Their children helped with the sewing and deliveries, and with the household chores that had to be done while Mother sewed.

RIGHT: Nathalie Rheinsberg married Julius Gumpertz, a fellow New York immigrant from Prussia, and by 1870 they were living at 97 Orchard Street. Julius was a shoemaker, but he had to take other work when steady employment became scarce. Like most married women of the time, Nathalie stayed at home and cared for their four young children, Rosa, Nannie, Olga, and baby Isaac.

Eight months after Julius disappeared, Isaac died of diarrhea, an all-too-common fate for nineteenth-century infants. Despite her sorrows, Nathalie managed to work and keep the family together.

RIGHT: The floral wallpaper in Nathalie's front room created a bright, cheerful mood for her work area. The lacy mantel cloth acted as both decoration and coverage (furniture in the late 1800s was often draped with fabric). Because her clients came to her for fittings, Nathalie would have placed her "best" belongings there as proof of her skill and success.

BELOW RIGHT: In 1883, Nathalie went to court to have her husband, who had been missing for nine years, declared legally dead. Her landlord, Lucas Glockner, testified at the successful hearing. After Julius disappeared, his father died, leaving his son $600 – an amount Nathalie inherited. Eventually, she moved from Orchard Street to Yorkville, on the Upper East Side. She died there in 1894. This remembrance card was given to the mourners at her funeral.

BELOW LEFT: Born nearly one hundred years after Nathalie's death, her great-great-great-grandchildren, Kasey and Dillon Reisman, reflect her image in the present.

Nathalie Gumpertz.

Died July 7th, 1894.
Aged 58 years.

Peaceful be thy silent slumber,
Peaceful in thy grave so low;
Thou no more will join our number,
Thou no more our sorrows know

Yet again we hope to meet thee,
When the day of life is fled;
Rad in Heaven with joy to greet thee,
Where no farewell tears are shed.

When Julius and Nathalie Gumpertz left Prussia (once a German state, now part of Poland) in the 1850s, they joined thousands of other immigrants who arrived in America and moved into the nearest, cheapest housing they could find. Many settled in the Lower East Side of Manhattan Island (originally called the East Side), which stretched from Fourteenth Street to Chambers Street, between the Bowery and the East River. When Dutch settlers first arrived in the 1620s, the area had been divided into eight farms. The map below, which is based on surveys made by an army officer named Bernard Ratzer in about 1767, already shows the area beginning to be more populated. The shipyards where some of the local residents worked can be seen at the bottom.

RIGHT: By 1700, the British had taken over New Amsterdam (later New York). Lt.-Gov. James De Lancey bought some of the East Side farmland and planned to develop a residential area there. During the American Revolution (1775–83), however, the De Lancey family backed the British instead of the Americans. Colonists like them were known as Loyalists, and after the war, their land was confiscated and sold to supporters of the revolution.

What became Orchard Street had once been the dirt road that led to the De Lancey orchard.

BELOW: By the 1830s, the streets of the Lower East Side were lined with wooden buildings that housed factories, home shops, and residences. The banks of the East River teemed with shipyards and slaughterhouses. Early Irish immigrants and African Americans were living and working in the poor Five Points area, where rents were low and amenities few. This period illustration displays both the variety of the early buildings and the hazards of living in such a notorious neighborhood.

ABOVE: Thousands of immigrants flooded into New York City in the middle to late 1800s. The newcomers sought out those who had come before them, the people who shared their language and customs and could help them establish their new life.

As these waves of immigrants from different countries moved into the Lower East Side, sections became known by the people who settled there. The Germans lived in Kleindeutschland (Little Germany), the Italians in Little Italy. As they prospered, people left the area, and the neighborhood changed to reflect the culture of the next group of new arrivals. Around 1900, Kleindeutschland was replaced by the Jewish Lower East Side. And so it continued.

ABOVE OPPOSITE: The original British homeowners moved away from the East Side in the late 1800s, and their modest two-story homes were soon subdivided and crammed with immigrants too poor to live elsewhere. These boardinghouses, each filled with as many as seventy people, were called rookeries.

BELOW OPPOSITE: In the twentieth century, immigrants have entered New York from the Caribbean and Southeast Asia, China and the Dominican Republic, the Philippines, Bangladesh, and Ecuador. Each group of new arrivals has brought its culture and traditions to the Lower East Side, transforming the area into a bridge between the past and the future.

Survival and economic success were the common goals of the millions of immigrants who arrived on America's shores. They fled from plague, famine, religious persecution, and war. Usually poor, they embarked on an ocean voyage carrying only a few belongings and their desire to live a better life, to be able to dream.

Life in America of the 1700s had to be carved out of a wilderness. With later land development and the growth of cities, however, immigrants began to arrive in greater numbers. Between 1840 and 1860, 4.5 million came, and the population of New York City doubled.

Before the state government became involved, the new arrivals were often the victims of swindlers, some of whom had themselves immigrated to America a short time before. These thieves met exhausted families at the docks, promising to carry their bags and help them find a place to live and a well-paying job, and then ran off with their belongings and cash. Someone had to protect the newcomers.

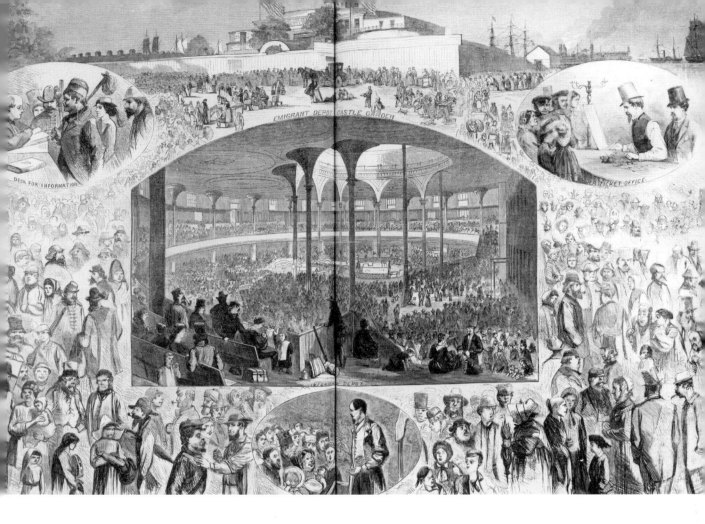

OPPOSITE: Mattresses, wooden crates, hatboxes, relatives, and travelers all crowd the docks as a steamer prepares to leave Germany for America. This *Harper's Weekly* magazine illustration captures the chaos and the noise. The artist draws our attention to the center of the picture, where a man flaps a handkerchief, a "flag" that waves good-bye to his old life. After about two weeks at sea, he will raise it again in joy when the ship arrives in New York.

BELOW RIGHT: In 1855, New York State officials began to use Castle Garden, an amusement hall at the edge of the harbor, as an immigrant receiving center. There the new arrivals were offered protection from swindlers. The huge American flag whipping the air and the open spaces of Battery Park were a welcome sight after the close quarters on board the steamer.

ABOVE: The services afforded the immigrants at the Castle Garden depot are featured in this period illustration. They could exchange their money for American currency, purchase railroad tickets, check job postings, or pick up messages from relatives who were waiting for them. Germans, Irish, Dutch, and Asians are drawn as ethnic caricatures that would have been considered appropriate during the late 1800s, when this picture was made. Castle Garden served as an immigration depot until 1890, when the federal government assumed full control of immigration.

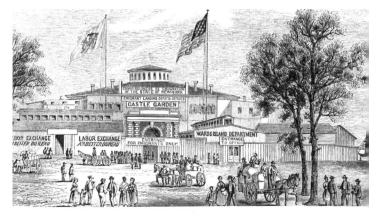

UNCLE SAM'S THANKSGIVING DINNER.

ABOVE: The expansion of America's cities and railroads led to a need for the low-cost labor that Europe and Asia could supply. Ads placed by American businesses encouraged people to leave the misery of their homelands for a happier life in the New World.

The image of the United States as a place where all the peoples of the world would be embraced is the subject of this illustration by Thomas Nast, a political cartoonist from the late 1800s. Uncle Sam carves the turkey for people from Ireland, Spain, China, Africa, and Germany. As at the first Thanksgiving, a Native American is sitting at the table. A picture of Castle Garden, a flag, and portraits of three presidents who supported freedom grace the wall. "Free and Equal," the cartoon proclaims – but Nast asks his observers to decide whether the newcomers really were all free and equal. Time would tell.

OPPOSITE: On October 28, 1886, the sculptor Frédéric Auguste Bartholdi pulled the veil from the face of a statue that would come to represent America to all the immigrants who sailed into New York harbor. A gift from France to the United States, *Liberty Enlightening the World*, as the Statue of Liberty was first known, was more than three hundred feet in total, making it the largest structure in New York. Immigrants nearing the harbor wept when they saw her, for she marked the end of one journey and the beginning of another.

Emma Lazarus, a descendant of Jewish immigrants to America, referred to Lady Liberty as "Mother of Exiles" in her poem "The New Colossus." In 1903, this poem was inscribed on a bronze plaque at Liberty's base, and its lines became familiar to many of the 14 million immigrants who sailed past the statue between 1886 and 1924, when new laws resulted in fewer arrivals.

"Give me your tired, your poor,

Your huddled masses yearning to breathe free,

The wretched refuse of your teeming shore.

Send these, the homeless, tempest-tost to me.

I lift my lamp beside the golden door!"

– Emma Lazarus

Although the Gumpertz family was processed at the Castle Garden depot, other tenants of 97 Orchard Street, like the Rogarshevskys (pages 32–35), were ferried from their steamer to the facilities on Ellis Island.

One in four Americans have a family connection to Ellis Island, which opened in 1892. The first station was built of wood and was used for only five years before it burned down in 1897. The rubble was cleared, and new brick buildings opened in December 1900. Much of the construction, including, for example, the tiled roof of the Registry Room, was done by immigrants who had arrived only a few years earlier.

OPPOSITE: The cheapest way to get to America was to travel in steerage, the part of the ship where the steering mechanism had once been located. Passengers wore tags that matched them to information on the ship's manifest, a list that identified all those on board. People who had never left their villages before were suddenly engulfed by thousands of strangers on the dock and on board.

In the early days of immigration, the voyage was hard: people couldn't change their clothes for weeks, and many were seasick. The stale air was filled with languages, sobs, and arguments caused by fear and frustration. Sometimes the steerage passengers were able to climb to the deck for fresh air and a chance to search the horizon for America.

ABOVE: Ellis Island was equipped to handle five thousand immigrants daily. By the early 1900s, however, an overwhelming twenty thousand people were arriving each day.

Groups of thirty people at a time moved into the Main Building, left their luggage, and were led to the stairs to the second floor. It was on these stairs that they were checked for any signs of ill health; their clothing was marked with blue chalk if further medical inspections were deemed necessary.

If the immigrants passed the stairway inspection, they moved into the crowded Registry Room at the top of the stairs for the final phase – questioning. The room buzzed with interpreters, examiners, and thousands of nervous, tired travelers who had to wait an average of five hours to be called up to an inspector's desk. Twenty-nine questions later, the immigrants walked down the Stairs of Separation behind the desk – one way for the detention room (and perhaps the news that they were going to be sent back home), another for the ferry or train ticket office, and yet another for the "kissing post," where many were met and embraced by joyous relatives.

BELOW: Ellis Island was officially closed in 1954; restrictive immigration laws had left it hardly used and too expensive to maintain. The buildings remained empty, ghostly relics in the harbor until restoration work returned the Main Building to its former beauty in 1990. Surviving pieces of copper ornamentation became the models for the restored domes.

ABOVE: Both emotionally drained and elated after their successful examination, these immigrants of 1907 await the ferry that will deliver them from Ellis Island to their new life. Many will have to travel by train for days in order to begin anew elsewhere in the country, where relatives may await them.

LEFT: The crowded conditions of the steamers, Ellis Island's Registry Room, and the New York harbor ferries were replaced for many weary newcomers by the crowded conditions of the Lower East Side's streets and buildings. The tall structures, built one against the other, amazed those people who had left country cottages surrounded by farmland and plenty of sky. The mountains of their former homelands had been exchanged for the piles of brick and metal that climb above the noisy streets to this day.

Victoria's dark braid slaps against her back as she runs up the stairs two at a time. The green cabbage falls from her hands, bounces down the stairs – bump-bump-bump – and rolls onto the dirty floor. Upstairs, her younger brother Jacob calls into the dark hallway from their apartment door. "Is that you, Victoria? Hurry!"

Victoria rubs the dust off the outer leaves of the wayward vegetable, the way she saw the push-cart man brush off the marks before he sold it to her. Then back up the stairs. It's time to make tasty *aromya*, pickled cabbage.

While little Salvator watches from his cot in the kitchen, Victoria and Jacob help Mrs. Confino cut and layer the cabbage in the huge crock. Cabbage, coarse salt, and vinegar. More cabbage, more salt, more vinegar. And then the cover and a weight are placed on top, pushing the cabbage down and keeping the air from getting in.

"The crock is crowded," says Jacob as Mrs. Confino slowly moves the container against the cool outside wall. "Like our rooms," adds Victoria, laughing, for ten people live in their apartment at 97 Orchard Street in 1916. The joke is funnier than she knows, for the word *aromya* is like a Spanish word for "piled up together."

OPPOSITE: After their comfortable home and successful grocery business in Kastoria, Greece, were destroyed by fire, Abraham and Rachel Confino immigrated to New York around 1914. There they joined their oldest daughter, Allegra, and her husband, Sam Russo. The Confinos' son Joe was also living in New York. Victoria, David, Saul, and Jacob accompanied their parents to Orchard Street. Two more children, Salvator and Esther, were born in America.

ABOVE: Victoria (circled) attended PS 65 on Hester Street until she was thirteen years old. Her father needed her help in the underwear factory he owned, and so Victoria's formal education came to an end, as happened with many young people. Within a few years,

she would become the wife of David Cohen through a marriage arranged by their parents.

RIGHT: The congested streets of the Lower East Side were dangerous, especially for small children. Lena, the first child of Allegra and Sam Russo, was born at 97 Orchard Street. One summer day in 1922, as Lena and her family waited to cross the busy street, a horse-pulled wagon passed by. Suddenly, the horse bolted, ran into the Russos, and killed Lena. She was only six years old.

OPPOSITE: Early tenants stumbled in an unlit hallway, but by the time Victoria Confino lived at number 97, gas fixtures lit the halls. As the codes and laws changed, so did the inside of the building. Fires were a constant terror of tenement life, and the hundreds of wooden steps were ready fuel. These decorative cast-iron treads (inset) were attached to each step when the building was "fireproofed." Such a remedy met the code but still didn't provide a safer exit in case of fire.

BELOW: When night fell, furniture did double duty in the Confino apartment. Makeshift beds were created from crates. A chair became the head and foot of another bed. *Mantas* (heavy shag rugs) were spread on the floor so that more people could sleep. If someone had to "go" in the middle of the night, it was much easier to use the room's chamber pot than to tiptoe through the snoring multitude.

ABOVE LEFT: Life was not all drudgery for the tenants of 97 Orchard Street. Victoria's family had a portable Victrola to play records. Trips to the local nickelodeon (a movie theater where tickets cost about five cents) were special treats. If a chaperone was available, Victoria could go to a dance hall. Mrs. Confino enjoyed her cigarettes and a game of poker, and Mr. Confino visited local Turkish coffeehouses with his friends.

ABOVE RIGHT: Irons and the ever-present water kettle sit on the Confinos' heavy stove. Water for cooking, laundry, and baths was heated on this stove.

The Confinos were Sephardic Jews who spoke Ladino (a language derived from Spanish, with Hebrew elements) and ate kosher foods. Sweet fritters called *boomuelos* were a favorite family dessert served at Passover.

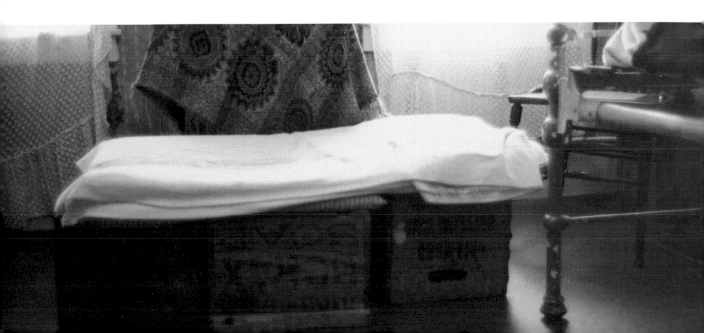

J ames De Lancey's property was bought and sold a number of times before the prosperous German immigrant Lucas Glockner built the tenement (apartment building) at 97 Orchard Street, between Broome and Delancey streets. Around 1800, Manhattan was reconfigured into standard-sized lots. The Orchard Street area was divided into parcels that measured 25 by 89 feet, and in 1814 the financier John Jacob Astor purchased four of these lots, including what would become 97 Orchard Street. Astor bought so much property, in fact, that he became the largest landowner in New York City.

In 1827, Astor sold three of his lots. By 1863, Lucas Glockner owned one, and the next year he moved his family into the brand-new five-story brick tenement building at 97 Orchard Street.

10th Ward 2d Sub District

ULE I.—CONSOLIDATED LIST of all persons of Class I, subject to do military duty in the _Fifth_ Congressional District, consisting of the Counties of _5th 10th 13th 14th_ Wards of the City and County of _New York_, State of _New York_, enumerated during the month of _May & June_, 1864 under direction of _Henry P. West Capt. &_, Provost Marshal.

comprises all persons subject to do military duty between the ages of twenty and thirty-five years, and all unmarried persons subject to do military duty above the age of thirty-five years and under the age of forty-five. Class II comprises all other persons subject to do military duty.

RESIDENCE		NAME	AGE 1st July, 1863.	WHITE OR COLORED.	PROFESSION, OCCUPATION, OR TRADE.	MARRIED OR UNMARRIED.	PLACE OF BIRTH. (Naming the State, Territory, or Country.)	FORMER MILITARY SERVICE.	REMARKS.	
Allen St	1	Seller William	25	W.	Foreman	Will	New York			1
" "	2	Green Daniel	20	"	Book Binder	Unm'd	Connecticut			2
" "	3	Geldner Frederick	43	"	Tassel Maker	M	Germany			3
" Rear	4	Goldschmidt Aaron	42	"	Cabinet Maker	"	"			4
Grand	5	Grace John	22	"	Cooper	Unm'd	Canada			5
" "	6	Grace Alexander	20	"	"	"	"			6
Division	7	Geisberg Frederick	25	"	Carver	"	Germany			7
" "	8	Geisberg William	22	"	Book Binder	"	"			8
Orchard	9	Glockner Lucas	44	"	Tailor	M'd	"			9
Browne	10	Gros William	43	"	Painter	"	"			10
Orchard	11	Girter John	40	"	Tailor	"	"			11
Delancey	12	Goal William	24	"	Jeweller	Unm.	"			12
Allen	13	Gaswat Gottlieb	20	"	Segar Maker	"	"			13
Eldridge	14	Gesser Michael	44	"	"	M	"			14
Bowery	15	Gall John	22	"	Waiter	Unm'd	Maryland			15
	16	Gengel Anton	26	"	Segar Maker	"	Germany			16
	17	Groeger Robert	38	"	Paper Bag Maker	M	"			17
	18	Gros Charles	35	"	Saloon Keeper	"	"			18
Orchard	19	Grundig Julius	36	"	Tassel Maker	"	"			19
" "	20	Glaser John	40	"	Shoe Maker	"	"			20

Colonel JAMES B. FRY, Provost Marshal General U.S., Washington, D.C.   STATION: Headquarters _5th_ Congr. Dist. of _New York State_   DATE: _____

OPPOSITE: John Jacob Astor was the embodiment of the immigrant's dream. He moved to America from Germany when he was twenty-one, arriving penniless. Within two years, he had earned enough money to open a small fur shop in New York City. Astor went on to create the American Fur Company and finance expeditions to establish trading posts in the West. When he died, he was the wealthiest person in America. More than 150 years later, he is still listed as the fourth-wealthiest person in American history.

ABOVE: There are no known portraits of landlord Lucas Glockner. His draft record of 1864 is one of the few documents that tells us about the builder and occupant of 97 Orchard Street. He is listed as forty-four years old, white, employed as a tailor, married, and of German birth. Such church, city, and military records provide researchers at the Lower East Side Tenement Museum with valuable historical data about the building's owners and tenants.

OPPOSITE: Unlike many landlords, Lucas Glockner moved his family into his building. Initially, a tenement was not the slum that the word now calls to mind, but was simply any building that was rented to three or more unrelated families. As the early rookeries were torn down and thousands of new immigrants poured into the East Side, more tenements like Glockner's were built.

Glockner's building provided him with the rental fees for nineteen apartments (his was the twentieth) and two basement-level commercial shops. He, his wife, Wilhelmina, and their three sons lived on Orchard Street until 1870, when they moved around the block to 25 Allen Street. There the Glockners' two daughters were born.

Lucas Glockner had a tailor shop to the left of the front stairs, or stoop. John Schneider owned a saloon in the other basement storefront. The saloon was a meeting place for local German immigrants. They could buy newspapers, hear about jobs, even do some banking. Glockner owned the building until 1886, and Schneider's saloon remained open until about 1885.

ABOVE: When the residents of 97 Orchard needed water or felt nature's call, they climbed down the many flights of stairs to the yard behind the building. There they found a spigot for drinking water. Nearby were the early privies (later models were called school sinks). Clothes flapped on lines strung from the building to the fence dividing the Orchard property from the similar small yards of other tenements.

The connected buildings and the fences left little open sky to enjoy and even less sunlight to dry the clothes. There were no lush lawns to play on or bushes and trees to attract birds and butterflies. The stench of the many outhouses on the block would have been overwhelming, even on a winter's day.

LIFE INSIDE NUMBER 97

Early residents of tenement buildings like 97 Orchard Street felt themselves fortunate to have a roof over their heads at a price they could barely afford (about seven to ten dollars a month in the early days). They lived in cramped, noisy quarters, with no amenities and little privacy. If there was an argument about money in the apartment next door, your family heard every word. If someone was dying or a baby was being born, you heard every moan. And day and night, there was the clomp-clomp of worn-out shoes going up and down the many flights of wooden stairs.

In the early years, there was no running water. If you wanted to cook something or wash up, you took a pail and filled it at the backyard tap. You ran outside to empty the slops and garbage. You had no refrigeration, so you ran up and down the stairs, in and out of the building, to purchase small amounts of food and drink – only as much as you could use before it spoiled (or more likely, as large an amount as you could afford).

It took a lot of energy and determination to live in a tenement.

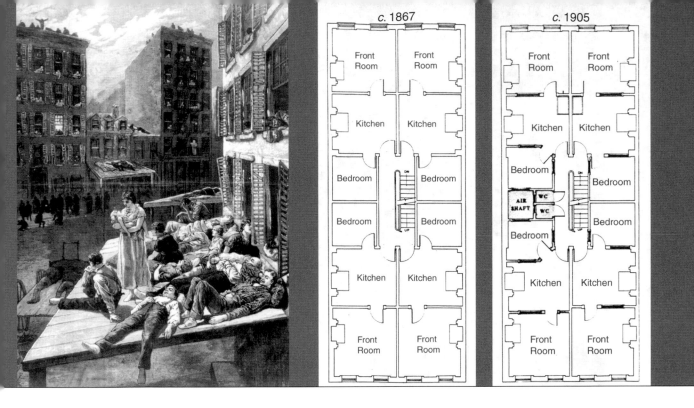

OPPOSITE: You entered your apartment through the front door, directly into the kitchen, often the busiest room. All the rooms (front room, kitchen, bedroom – about 325 square feet in total) were connected by doors, rather than a hallway. The largest room, the front room, was only 11 by 12 1/2 feet.

Before gas was installed at 97 Orchard Street around 1900, the rooms were lit by candles or kerosene lamps. The stove and fireplaces were the only sources of heat, and that bit of warmth seldom reached the bedroom, where the children or boarders usually slept.

ABOVE LEFT: Before more windows were added in 1905, inside rooms had no access to air or light. On hot summer nights, tenants often moved to the roofs, porches, or fire escapes of their buildings to get some relief from the heat. In this late 1880s illustration, people are silhouetted against the night sky on every available rooftop, window, and porch. With the dawn, they will return to the oppressive heat indoors or on the streets.

ABOVE RIGHT: These two floor plans illustrate the general layout of New York ten-ement buildings such as 97 Orchard Street, as well as the structural changes that eventually improved the tenants' lives.

The New York State Tenement House Act of 1867 provided regulations for building owners to follow. Another housing act, passed in 1879 and called the Old Law, meant that no more tenements like Glockner's would be built. Rooms had to open to the street, yard, or an air shaft, and more natural light had to be allowed to enter the building. The resulting new design was called a dumbbell apartment because that piece of exercise equipment was what the building looked like from above.

In 1901, the passage of yet another tenement house law (called the New Law) meant that major changes finally had to be made to 97 Orchard Street. Real, flushable gas-lit toilets had to be installed, one for every two apartments. By 1905, the tenants also had two fireproof air shafts (which unfortunately made the small bedrooms even smaller) and windows in all the partition walls. The law, however, did not require a landlord to install electricity, so the tenants at number 97 had to wait until about 1924 to be able to switch on light bulbs.

ABOVE: This immigrant family sits in a kitchen similar to those at 97 Orchard Street. Two or three families might have lived together in this apartment. The two youngest will share the baby crib. The bed serves as a couch during the day. The interior window brings light and heat into the bedroom, where the clothes hang on hooks. A kettle sits on the gas burner, and the family's few belongings are arranged in the shallow cupboard.

LEFT: In 1905, indoor toilets were welcomed by the tenants of 97 Orchard Street, who for years had been scrambling to the backyard privies. There was little privacy in the new facilities, however, and every flush could be heard by the tenants. Scraps of old newspaper served as toilet tissue.

OPPOSITE: Both Mrs. Baldizzi (pages 46–49) and Mrs. Rogarshevsky (pages 32–35) were known as excellent housekeepers who kept their apartments and meager belongings incredibly clean. Such cleaning would have been difficult and never-ending.

Coal and wood in the tenements meant soot and dust collected everywhere. The crowded streets and local manufacturers added to the pollution, and residents of Orchard Street also had to contend with the dirt tossed up by the elevated rail track that ran along nearby Allen Street.

These children are sitting on an Allen Street fire escape in 1916. The sheets and coverlets are providing either shade from the heat or a "tree house" on the tree-less street. To the left is the elevated train track, close enough for the children to wave to the passengers.

Outside 97 Orchard Street the vendors call out to prospective buyers. Noisy children, out of school for the summer, run into grumpy shoppers and circle buggies filled with cranky babies. It's July 1918. A group of men sit on the stoop and speak of the war now raging in Europe, in the very homelands they left for America.

Inside the dark building, visitors' hard heels clip against the metal stair treads as they climb to the Rogarshevsky apartment. They kiss their fingers and touch the mezuzah, a small prayer case attached to the door frame, thus showing their respect for God. The curtains are drawn. The red parlor is stuffy.

Fannie Rogarshevsky and her sons Sam, twenty, and Henry, sixteen, are sitting shiva, a seven-day mourning period. After a two-year battle with tuberculosis, Abraham, their husband and father, has died. He spent the last weeks of his life coughing in the airless bedroom. He was only forty-five.

"May the Eternal comfort you among the other mourners of Zion and Jerusalem," repeat the visitors to the mourning family. Out in the backyard, children scream with delight as they drench each other with cooling water from the tap and slip on the muddy ground.

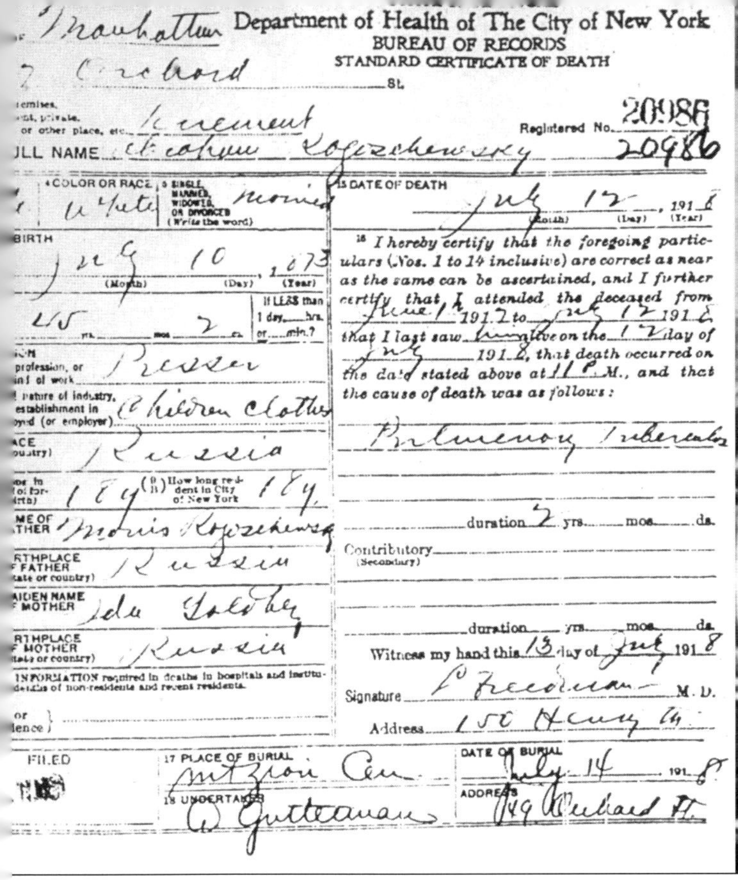
Manhattan Department of Health of The City of New York
BUREAU OF RECORDS
STANDARD CERTIFICATE OF DEATH

97 Orchard St.

Tenement

Registered No. 20986

FULL NAME Abraham Rogoschewsky 20986

COLOR OR RACE White | SINGLE, MARRIED, WIDOWED, OR DIVORCED (Write the word) married

DATE OF DEATH July 12 1918 (Month) (Day) (Year)

BIRTH July 10 1873 (Month) (Day) (Year)

45 yrs. 2 mos. ... If LESS than 1 day, ...hrs. or ...min.?

I hereby certify that the foregoing particulars (Nos. 1 to 14 inclusive) are correct as near as the same can be ascertained, and I further certify that I attended the deceased from June 1 1912 to July 12 1918 that I last saw h... alive on the 12 day of July 1918, that death occurred on the date stated above at 11 P. M., and that the cause of death was as follows:

Pulmonary Tuberculosis

duration 2 yrs. ... mos. ... ds.

Contributory (Secondary) ...

duration ... yrs. ... mos. ... ds.

Witness my hand this 13 day of July 1918

Signature L. Freedman M. D.

Address 150 Henry St.

profession, or kind of work Presser

nature of industry, establishment in ... (or employer) Children clothes

BIRTHPLACE (country) Russia

How long resident in City of New York 18 y.

NAME OF FATHER Moris Rogoschewsky

BIRTHPLACE OF FATHER (State or country) Russia

MAIDEN NAME OF MOTHER Ida Toloky

BIRTHPLACE OF MOTHER (State or country) Russia

INFORMATION required in deaths in hospitals and institutions of non-residents and recent residents.

FILED

PLACE OF BURIAL Mt. Zion Cem.

DATE OF BURIAL July 14 1918

UNDERTAKER W. Gutterman

ADDRESS 149 Orchard St.

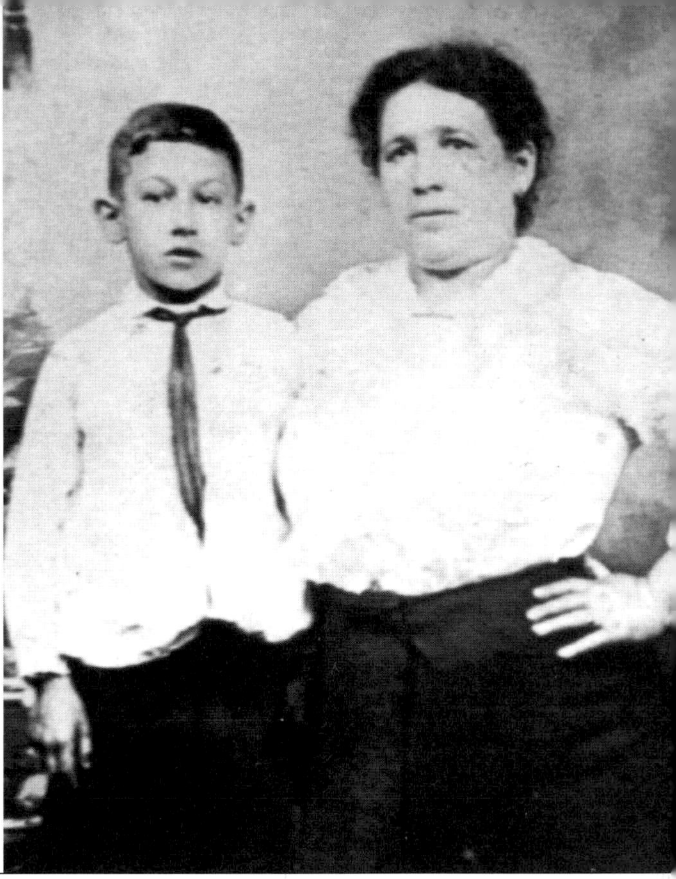

OPPOSITE: Abraham and Fannie Rogarshevsky emigrated from Lithuania to New York in 1901. They brought their three daughters, two sons, and an infant niece, whom they raised. By the time the family moved to Orchard Street, one daughter had died and two more sons had been born. Two daughters had married and moved out by 1915 – and the "extra" space had been rented to a boarder. Fannie's parents, the Bayards, also lived in the building.

ABOVE LEFT: Some members of the Rogarshevsky family worked in the garment industry. Abraham toiled long hours as a presser in a garment shop. Some pressers heated heavy hand irons and used them until they cooled down and could no longer remove wrinkles or flatten seams. These irons were placed on the stoves to reheat and exchanged for ones that had already been warmed up. This rotation of hot irons continued all day, and probably into the night. The lack of fresh air and sunshine no doubt added to Abraham's miseries.

Historical records, like this death certificate, provide information about Abraham. Here we see he worked in the "children['s] clothes" industry. The page also provides his parents' names, his age, how long he was in the United States, and his place of burial.

ABOVE RIGHT: Like many immigrants, the Rogarshevskys made their names more "American." For instance, Estr, Bosse, Moishe, Scholem, and Rafael became Ida, Bessie, Morris, Sam, and Philip. Rogarshevsky had become Rosenthal by 1925.

After Abraham's death, Fannie became the custodian for the building, scrubbing the halls, toilets, and stairs. In this way, she was able to support herself and the children who still lived at home.

Although the rest of the building was closed in 1935, Fanny continued to live in her apartment with her son Philip (seen above in about 1919) and his wife, Miriam, until 1941, when they moved to the Vladeck Houses, new public housing in New York. The Rosenthals were the last family to live at 97 Orchard Street.

ABOVE: The open interior window allowed light and air to flow into the Rogarshevskys' cramped kitchen. At night, the neat stack of linens will be put to use as the kitchen becomes a much-needed extra "bedroom."

ABOVE OPPOSITE: A mourning meal was provided for the people who visited while the Rogarshevsky family sat shiva. Round foods, like these oranges, buns, and eggs, were served because they represented the circle, or cycle, of life and death. Boys younger than thirteen and girls younger than twelve could not participate, so Abraham and Fannie's son Philip, who was only eleven, did not join the group.

BELOW OPPOSITE: In keeping with Jewish custom, the mirrors throughout the apartment were covered for about a week after Abraham's death. On top of the dresser in his bedroom there was a lamp (needed day and night because of the darkness of the room), grooming materials, and glass cups called *bankes*. These last items were heated inside and applied to the body. It was believed that illness could be drawn out of a body by "cupping." When the cups had been on for the required period, they were removed, making the popping sound of a suction cup.

In 1903, the Tenement Commission of New York stated that the city block on which 97 Orchard Street sits had more than two thousand residents and was the most crowded block in the city, some said the world. And still the immigrants, in transit from the Old World to the New, poured into New York and sought shelter.

Between 1863 and 1935, at least seven thousand people from more than twenty countries lived in the tenement that Lucas Glockner built. Thousands of others – relatives, doctors, the building's various owners – walked through the sturdy front door and stepped into the dim hallway. These are just some of those people.

OPPOSITE: *Circa* 1904. Cherry Danzig, the daughter of a furniture dealer, was born at number 97 in April 1901. A few years later, her hair adorned with perky bows, she steadies herself against the back of a carved bench in a photographer's studio. Her brother, Abraham, dressed in a child's gown (as was the custom for infant boys and girls), nestles against the tapestry.

BELOW RIGHT:

Circa 1916. Mr. and Mrs. Philip Tereshko are living at number 97. Only three years before, they posed for this wedding portrait. They look  intensely at the photographer. Perhaps the watch pinned to her breast is a wedding gift. Perhaps the roses are artificial, made by homeworkers in tenements like those on Orchard Street.

ABOVE LEFT: *Circa* 1920. With wrinkly stockings and bobbed hair, the Elias sisters, Esther, Lillian, and Estelle, look wistfully into the camera. Are they frightened or curious?

ABOVE RIGHT: *Circa* 1938. Rose Bonofiglio attends the confirmation of her goddaughter, Josephine Baldizzi. The Bonofiglio and Baldizzi families met when they both lived at 97 Orchard Street, a few years before this church ceremony. Because many immigrants had left their closest relatives in their native lands, new friends in America became surrogate relations.

PRICE, 15c
AND UP
97 Orchard Street,

Bet. Delancy & Broome Sts.   1st Fl. Back, Room 4, N. Y.

The World Famous Palmist and Mind Reader
recently arrived from Europe.

PROF. DORA MELTZER,

She guesses the name and age of Every Person

She is an unexcelled
Palmist, tells you the
past, present and future
gives the best advice in
business, journeys, Law
Suits, Love, Sickness, Family
affairs, etc.

Open from 9 A. M. to 10 P. M.
97 Orchard Street,

Bet. Delancy & Broome Sts.   1st Fl. Back, Room 4, N.

OPPOSITE: Around 1905, some cosmetic changes were made in the hallway of 97 Orchard Street. If the mansions on Fifth Avenue could have fancy trimmings, then so too could the tenements. Woodwork was painted to look like more expensive timber. Varnished burlap was applied to the cracked walls, and colorful country scenes were added. Finally, plaster "frosting" squeezed from a bag created scrollwork that danced across the walls.

ABOVE LEFT: Generations of wires and pipes snaked around the moldings and brought water and electricity to the grateful tenants.

ABOVE RIGHT: Some of the visitors at number 97 looked for answers from Prof. Dora Meltzer, who lived and worked in "1st floor back, Room 4" around 1890. An advertisement for her business was discovered under the floorboards during restoration. Practitioners of so-called sciences like palmistry and phrenology (reading the bumps on a person's head) offered consolation to people who were miserable, hopeful, and had the fifteen cents to hear what they wanted to hear.

I n an area as crowded as the Lower East Side, there were plenty of activities for photographers to record. This sampling of images provides glimpses into the work and play of new Americans like those on Orchard Street.

OPPOSITE: A mother shops for the day's groceries. As she hurries along the sidewalk, her daughters clutch at her skirt so they won't get lost. A peddler, patiently awaiting his next sale, sits on a crate. Polished vegetables threaten to tumble from a grocer's stand. Oh, what was that?

ABOVE: The power of some photographs leads us to ask questions. What is this boy's name? Is that his dog, distracted by something in the gutter? Why are the boy's shoes

so big? Did he ever leave the Lower East Side for a better life?

During the early 1900s, children as young as five worked. They transported bundles of clothing to their homes for finishing and then trudged back to the manufacturer with the completed work. This solemn boy carries home a hefty load of unfinished clothing. During the winter months, some families used the wool garment pieces as extra bed coverings until the work was returned.

ABOVE: The American author Nathaniel Hawthorne looks down upon young readers at the East Broadway branch of the Aguilar Free Library. Everyone looks very engrossed in their books – but a few children are watching the photographer.

ABOVE OPPOSITE: As the laundry dries in the cool air, children play on improvised seesaws and swings in tenement backyards. Mothers chat while keeping an eye on the playmates. Big sister helps the baby down into a sandbox that doesn't have any sand.

Beautiful Seward Park opened nearby in 1901. It provided the neighborhood children with separate play areas for girls and boys, and with grass, trees, and flowers that were lacking on their home streets. At first, parents didn't like the park. Mothers were used to glancing out their windows and seeing their children in the backyards. Gradually, however, they came to enjoy it.

BELOW LEFT: Health and cleanliness were topics discussed with mothers when the visiting nurse came to call. Many tenement residents did not have bathtubs – some went to the local public bathhouses and paid a few cents to bathe. In areas as overcrowded as the Lower East Side, outbreaks of cholera, influenza, and tuberculosis were feared.

BELOW RIGHT: On May 9, 1896, a photographer snapped this picture of a neighborhood policeman and a street sweeper, both sporting the lush mustaches so fashionable at the time. The elevated train tracks loom in the background.

A sweeper had plenty to collect – the droppings from the many horses and the garbage that accumulated after a day of pushcart sales on the streets.

DRASTIC CHANGES

In the 1920s, new laws severely restricted the number of immigrants who were allowed into the United States. The Johnson-Reed Act of 1924 permitted only about 150,000 new arrivals a year, a trickle compared to the massive influx earlier in the century. Fewer immigrants meant less crowded conditions in tenement neighborhoods, but times were still tough for those who remained. Local businesses closed and unemployment grew as the Great Depression took hold.

New laws meant that building owners had to make expensive renovations to their old buildings to modernize them. The changes would be costly, but tenants couldn't afford to pay more rent. The solution for many owners was to evict their tenants and board up their buildings. That's what the owner of 97 Orchard Street did in 1935. Only the shops on the two bottom floors remained open. While life continued outside, the upper stories of number 97 slept undisturbed for more than fifty years.

OPPOSITE: Owning a pushcart was one way to eke out a living. Cart owners didn't need much, just a bit of produce or a few pairs of shoes. There was no rent, and they could roll the cart home at the end of the day. It was difficult to sit out on rainy or steamy days, but at least the owners had control over hours and goods, and didn't have to answer to an employer.

ABOVE LEFT: Fiorello H. La Guardia was the mayor of New York from 1933 until 1945. He understood what immigrant life was like. He had grown up in a tenement building, which he called a "rat hole," and when he was a young man, he worked as an interpreter at Ellis Island. He wanted to make drastic changes to the tenement system – and he did. Tenement buildings were demolished and new homes for the less fortunate, called public housing projects, were constructed.

ABOVE RIGHT: In the 1930s, fifteen thousand pushcarts filled the Lower East Side streets. They blocked the paths of fire engines and rescue equipment. They also made it difficult for the growing number of trucks and automobiles to travel through the area. In 1938, during Mayor La Guardia's administration, pushcarts were banned.

The Essex Street Market was built to take the place of the carts; vendors could rent space inside. But many cart owners couldn't afford to open for business in the market. For a time, unhappy customers refused to shop indoors.

BELOW: Even the city's entertaining organ grinders were banned from walking the streets, making music. Here the owners line up to turn in their popular instruments.

"Are they asleep yet, ZaZa?" Adolfo Baldizzi whispers to his wife. "I'll see," Rosaria softly replies, and she tiptoes through the kitchen, her shoes sliding across the linoleum floor. She stands quietly for a moment, peeking into the bedroom.

Eight-year-old Josephine and her younger brother, Johnny, are sound asleep, stretched out head to toe on the folding bed. Rosaria returns to the front room. Even the canary is asleep. She signals to Adolfo that all's well, and he opens the window to let in Christmas, 1934.

During his walks through the neighborhood looking for work as a handyman, Adolfo has been collecting pine boughs for this very night. From the fire escape, he brings in the sticky branches and begins to make a Christmas tree. His sturdy tool box provides the tacks and wire he needs, and the "tree" is soon attached to the wall.

Rosaria moves about the cold room, dusting off the trunk and the dresser. She brushes at invisible dirt on the picture of Our Lady of Perpetual Help, making the sign of the cross as she does. Then, as if by magic, she produces several bright oranges and places them under the tree.

All is ready. It's time to go to bed. In just a few hours, the dawn's light will seep through the lace curtains, the canary will sing, and it will be the Christ child's birthday.

Rosaria turns to kiss her husband goodnight. "Merry Christmas," she says.

"*Buon natale*, my ZaZa," Adolfo whispers in the dark.

OPPOSITE: Adolfo Baldizzi and Rosaria Mutolo were born on the island of Sicily. Adolfo served as a soldier in the First World War and married Rosaria in 1922. By 1924, they were living in America.

ABOVE: Rosaria (second from right) worked in a garment factory for many years. After the Second World War began in 1939, Adolfo worked in the shipyards. The family's increased income meant they could move out of the Lower East Side and across the river to Brooklyn, where they spent the rest of their lives.

BELOW LEFT: Josephine and Johnny shared the bed in the tiny third room. Every morning, they folded it up and draped it with a fabric cover Rosaria had made. This gave them just a bit more room to play.

Josephine decorated the room with pictures of glamorous movie stars, including Katharine Hepburn (left) and Joan Crawford. She also liked to dress up in her mother's "best clothes" – when her parents were not at home.

BELOW RIGHT: Rosaria was referred to as "Shine 'Em Up Sadie" by those who knew how clean she kept her small apartment. In 1935, the cracked linoleum rug was scrubbed one last time. The Baldizzis, like all the other families evicted from 97 Orchard Street, had to pack up their few belongings and find another home on nearby Eldridge Street.

ABOVE LEFT: In the window, Adolfo Baldizzi's blue morning glories basked in the sunlight. Although he was a skilled carpenter and craftsman, Adolfo had had trouble finding work during the Great Depression. The family received aid through the Home Relief program, which provided wooden boxes of cheese, among other items. Adolfo recycled the boxes into window planters that cheered not only the family, but also any passersby who glanced up.

ABOVE RIGHT: In 1993, Josephine Baldizzi visited her childhood home at 97 Orchard Street. She recalled watching for her neighbor, Mrs. Rosenthal, at the bedroom window opposite hers on Friday evenings. Jewish custom decreed that Mrs. Rosenthal could not turn on the lights on the Sabbath. When she waved across the air shaft, Josephine would go next door to do the job for her.

OPPOSITE: In 2001, her husband, children, and grandchildren returned to the apartment to remember Josephine (who had died in 1998) and share the story of Adolfo and Rosaria. (Front row, left to right: son Roger, granddaughter Gina; back row, left to right: daughter Maria, grandson James, husband George, grandson Roger.)

In 1988, the lights shone once again inside gloomy 97 Orchard Street. Ruth J. Abram had a vision for what would become the first tenement in the United States to be transformed into a museum. Her search with Anita Jacobson for a suitable building resulted in the purchase of the Orchard Street site. Research showed that residents from more than twenty countries had lived there. Some of their stories were revealed through the urban archeology conducted on the premises over the next few years.

During restoration, more than fifteen hundred artifacts were found. Backyard digging yielded information about the toilet system, and interviews with former residents gave Abram and her staff valuable insights into life inside the building. Gradually, through diligent research and patient attention to detail, the first two family apartments were recreated and opened to the public in 1994. Since then, continued efforts have seen two more apartments restored, and the recreation work continues.

The Museum is an affiliate of the National Trust for Historic Preservation and the National Park Service and is linked with other important immigration sites, including Ellis Island, the Statue of Liberty, and Castle Clinton. It is also the first tenement building to be designated a National Historic Landmark.

While the Lower East Side Tenement Museum interprets the immigrant community of the past, it is also strongly committed to the present and the future. The area continues to be the first home for many immigrants to America. Often these newcomers live in crowded tenements, work long hours in factories, and struggle to get by in a new land, just as the former residents of 97 Orchard Street did. These people are partners in the Museum's work. Classes for new arrivals draw on the stories of earlier immigrants to teach English and life skills. Students are surprised to learn how similar their experiences are to those of the Rogarshevsky and Baldizzi families. They are encouraged to write their own stories, become active in the community, and help the latest arrivals adapt to their own new lives. Thousands of schoolchildren also take part each year in programs that make them aware of life then and now, and the role they too can play in the future of their communities.

The Museum's staff and volunteers are eager to see historic sites around the world change from places of passive history-telling to ones of "engagement for citizenship." The Lower East Side Tenement Museum is a museum with conscience, a place that uses history to promote citizenship, community spirit, and tolerance.

Orchard Street teems with faces and
voices of the world.
The steamy air is full of quick questions and
hasty replies.
"How much?"
"Too much!"
"What size?"
"How much did you say?"
Baskets and skirts and cabbages and
bags and decorations and dollar bills
rustle
and the shadows grow longer,
stretching from the past to the present.

52

The old suitcase yawns,
waiting to be filled for the voyage
across the ocean,
across the street,
across the country.
From an old life to a new one,
from the New World back to the Old
for a visit.
Shirts, too few not to cherish,
have grown into racks upon racks,
neatly labeled and tagged,
like the suitcase.

THE LOWER EAST SIDE TENEMENT MUSEUM

Visitors' Center:
90 Orchard Street, New York, NY 10002
(corner of Orchard and Broome)

Business Office:
66 Allen Street, New York, NY 10002
Phone: (212) 431-0233

For further information about the Museum (hours, ticket prices, and programs), visit www.tenement.org.

ACKNOWLEDGMENTS

Heartfelt thanks are extended by the author and the photographer to Ruth J. Abram, President of the Lower East Side Tenement Museum, and the Museum staff: Steve Long, Curator; Vincent Lenza, Collections Manager; Katherine E. Snider, Vice President of Public Affairs; Kate Fermoile, Director of Education; Benjamin Trimmier, Marketing and PR Associate; and Linda Pankiewicz and Rebecca Hinde, Museum Guides. The author also thanks Michele G. Rubin of Writers House LLC; David Bennett of Transatlantic Literary Agency Inc; Eleanor W. Gillers of the New-York Historical Society; the Statue of Liberty-Ellis Island Foundation, Inc.; and Cal Smiley, who welcomed an immigrant into his life. Finally, both offer their sincere gratitude to the Tundra Books staff: Kathy Lowinger, Catherine Mitchell, Lynn Paul, Sue Tate, Tamara Sztainbok, Janice Weaver, and Kong Njo.

PHOTO CREDITS

All photographs are by Arlene Alda, with the exception of the following:
Page 1: Johnny and Josephine Baldizzi on the roof of 97 Orchard Street, Lower East Side Tenement Museum (hereafter LESTM) FPA 9901.7; 5, bottom: LESTM FPA 9919.1; 6, lower left: LESTM FPA 9911; lower right: LESTM; 8: collection of the New-York Historical Society (hereafter NYHS) 56838; 9, top: NYHS 32994; bottom: LESTM PA 9901.13; 10: LESTM PA 9907.15; 11, top: LESTM PA 9901.17; 12: LESTM PA 9901.34a; 13, top: NYHS 48757; bottom: NYHS 21159A; 14: LESTM PA 9901.23a; 16: LESTM PA 9903.6–National Parks Service/Ellis Island Immigration Museum; 19: courtesy of the Museum of the City of New York (hereafter MCNY); 20: LESTM FPA 9903.21; 21, top: LESTM FPA 9903.9a; bottom: LESTM FPA 9903.20; 24: NYHS 35284; 25: LESTM FPA 9909.1; 26: LESTM PA 9908.30 (model made by Dan Castelli); 27: LESTM PA 9908.12a; 29, top left: LESTM PA 9901.6a; top right: LESTM; 30, top: courtesy of MCNY, the Jacob A. Riis Collection #502; 31: courtesy of MCNY 31.93.14; 32: LESTM FPA 9914; 33, left: LESTM FPA 9914.15; right: LESTM FPA 9914.2; 36: LESTM FPA 9904.5; 37, top left: LESTM FPA 9906.3; top right: LESTM FPA 9901.2; bottom: LESTM FPA 9918.1; 39, right: LESTM FPA 9923.1e; 40: source unknown; 41: courtesy of Brown Brothers; 42: courtesy of the New York Public Library Archives, the New York Public Library, Astor, Lenox and Tilden Foundations; 43, top: LESTM/New York City Police Department; bottom left: courtesy of Metropolitan Life Insurance Company; bottom right: Alice Austen Collection, the Staten Island Historical Society, New York; 44: LESTM OPA 9903.36/Children's Aid Society 24-0888; 45, top left: courtesy of MCNY, Print Archives; top right: LESTM PA 9903.10/69–National Archives ANP-8-P3032.135; bottom: courtesy MCNY; 46, left: LESTM FPA 9901; right: LESTM FPA 9901; 47, top: LESTM FPA 9901.8a; 48, right: LESTM; 50: LESTM; 51, top right: LESTM, photo by Benjamin Epps; middle: LESTM, painting by Maggie Zander; 52, top: courtesy of MCNY, the Byron Collection; 53, top: LESTM PA 9910.4.